D1153780

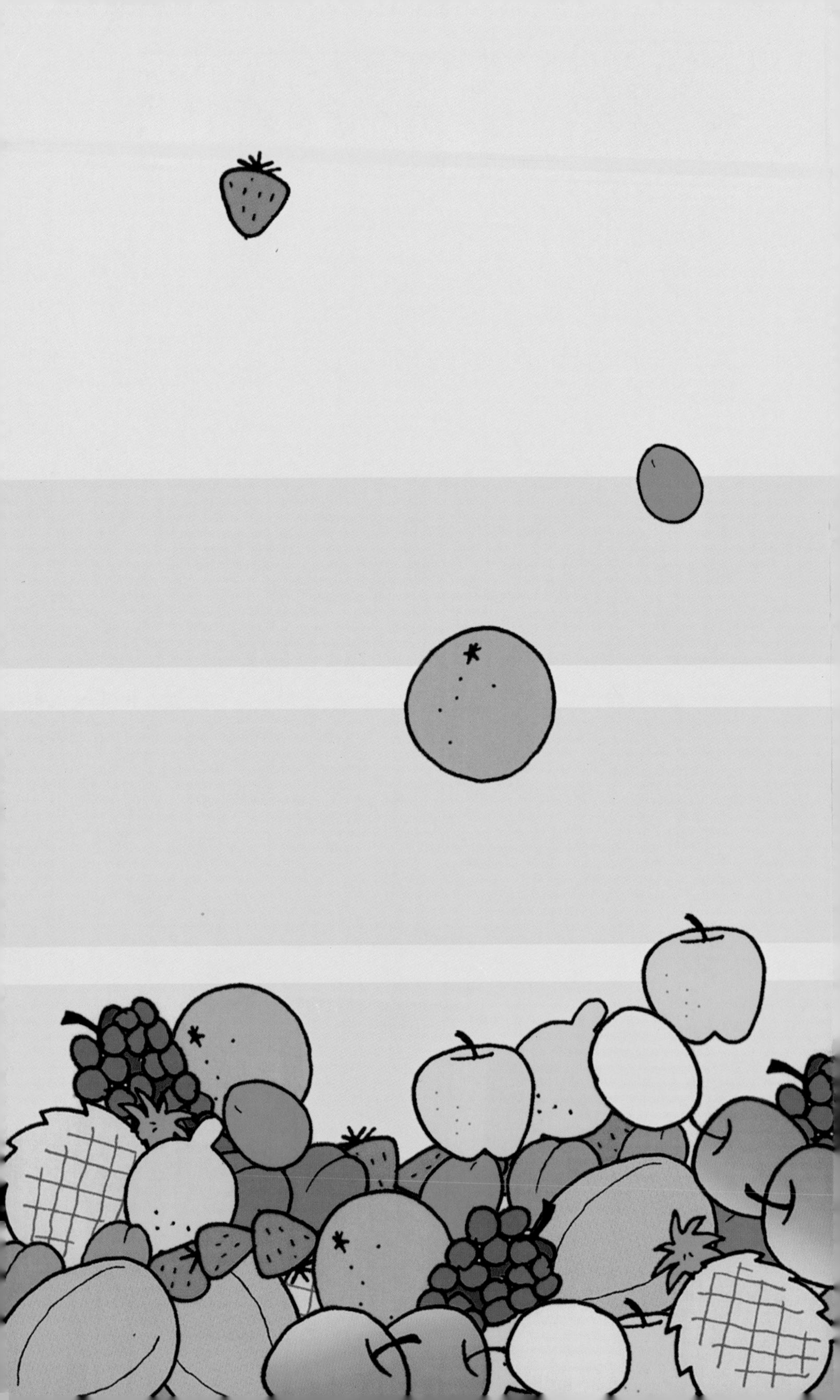

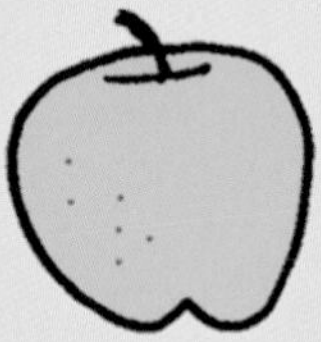
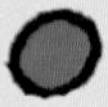
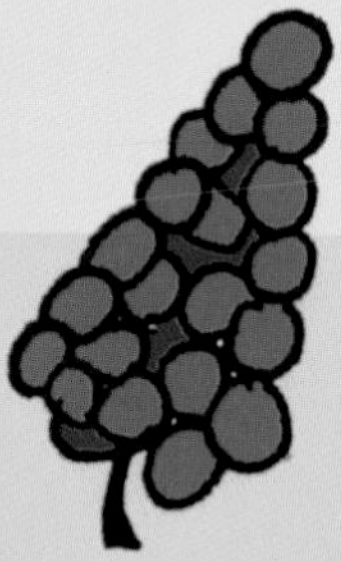
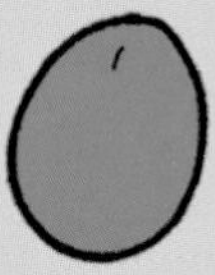
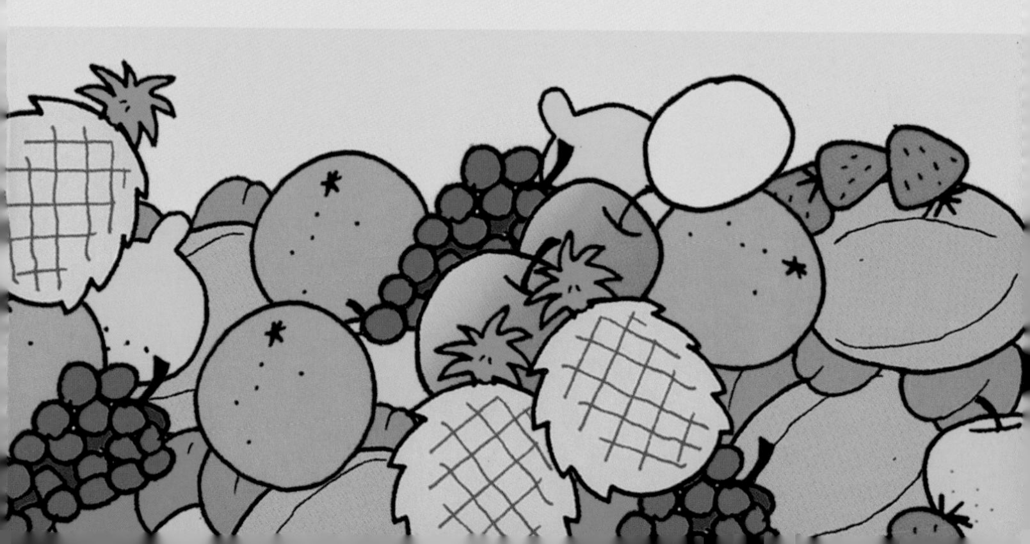

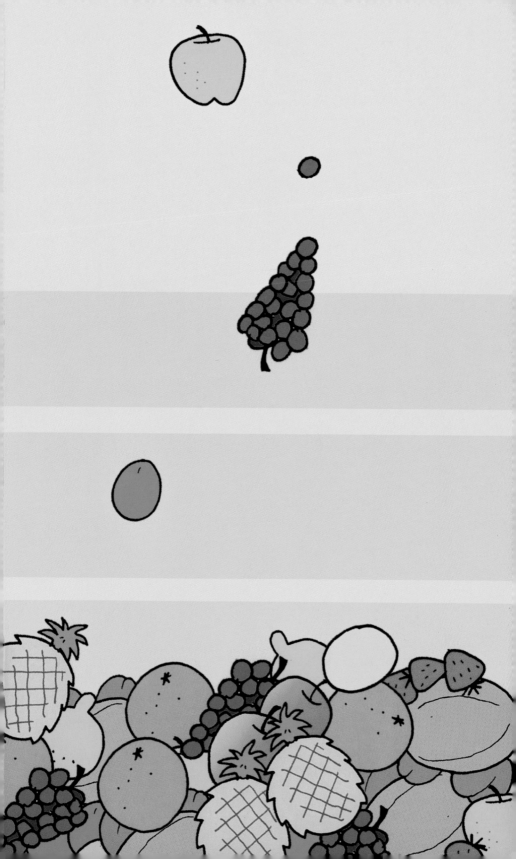

FIRST GRAPHICS

MyPlate and Healthy Eating

The Fantastic Fruit Group

BY MARCIE ABOFF

ILLUSTRATED BY GARY SWIFT

Consultant: Amy Lusk, MS, RD, LD
Registered Dietitian
Nationwide Children's Hospital, Columbus, Ohio

CAPSTONE PRESS
a capstone imprint

First Graphics are published by Capstone Press,
151 Good Counsel Drive, P.O. Box 669, Mankato, Minnesota 56002.
www.capstonepub.com

Books published by Capstone Press are manufactured with paper
containing at least 10 percent post-consumer waste.

Library of Congress Cataloging-in-Publication Data
Aboff, Marcie.
  The fantastic fruit group / by Marcie Aboff ; illustrated by Gary Swift.
    p. cm.—(First graphics. MyPlate and healthy eating)
  Summary: "Simple text and illustrations present MyPlate and the
fruit group, the foods in this group, and examples of healthy eating
choices"—Provided by publisher.
  Includes bibliographical references and index.
  ISBN 978-1-4296-6090-7 (library binding)
  ISBN 978-1-4296-7160-6 (paperback)
  1. Fruit—Juvenile literature. I. Swift, Gary, ill. II. Title.
QK660.A26 2012
581.4'64—dc22
                              2011002447

Editorial Credits
Lori Shores, editor; Juliette Peters, designer; Nathan Gassman, art director;
    Eric Manske, production specialist

Image Credits
USDA/MyPlate.com 4, (MyPlate icon)

Serving sizes are based on recommendations for children ages 4 through 8.

Printed in the United States of America in Stevens Point, Wisconsin.
032011   006240F11

Table of Contents

The Fruit Group

Everyone has a favorite food.

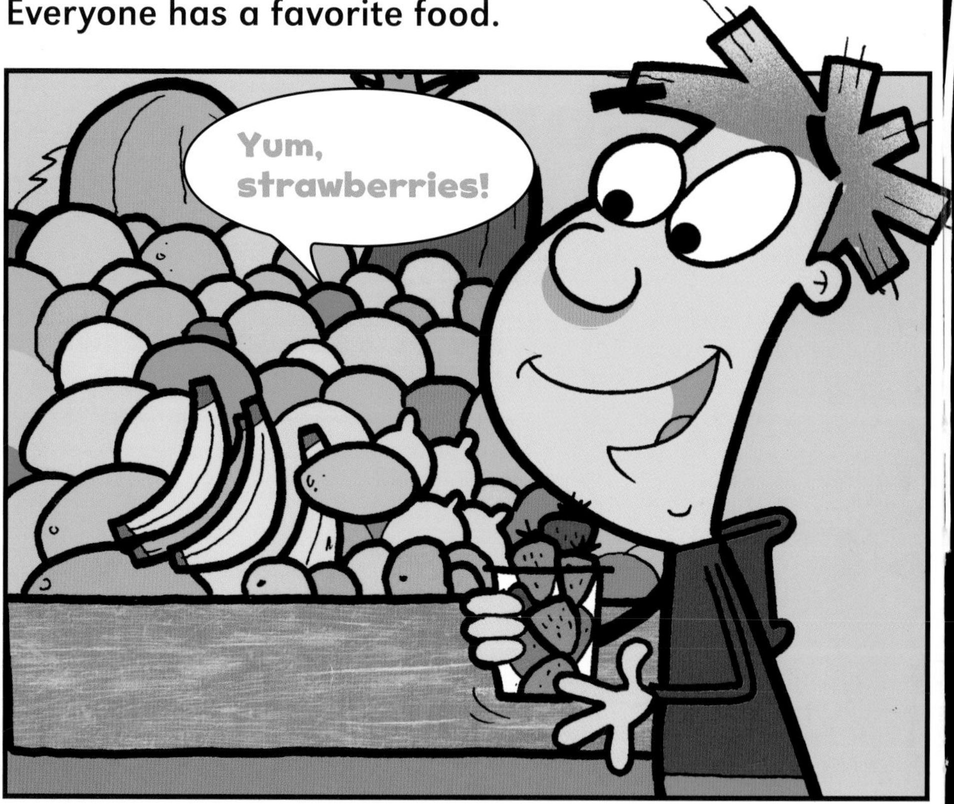
Yum, strawberries!

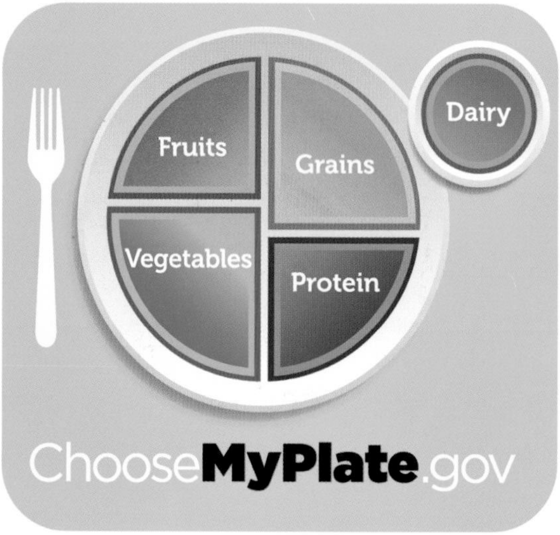
Dairy
Fruits
Grains
Vegetables
Protein
ChooseMyPlate.gov

All of your favorite foods have a place on MyPlate.

MyPlate is a guide for healthy eating. It shows how much you need from each of the five food groups.

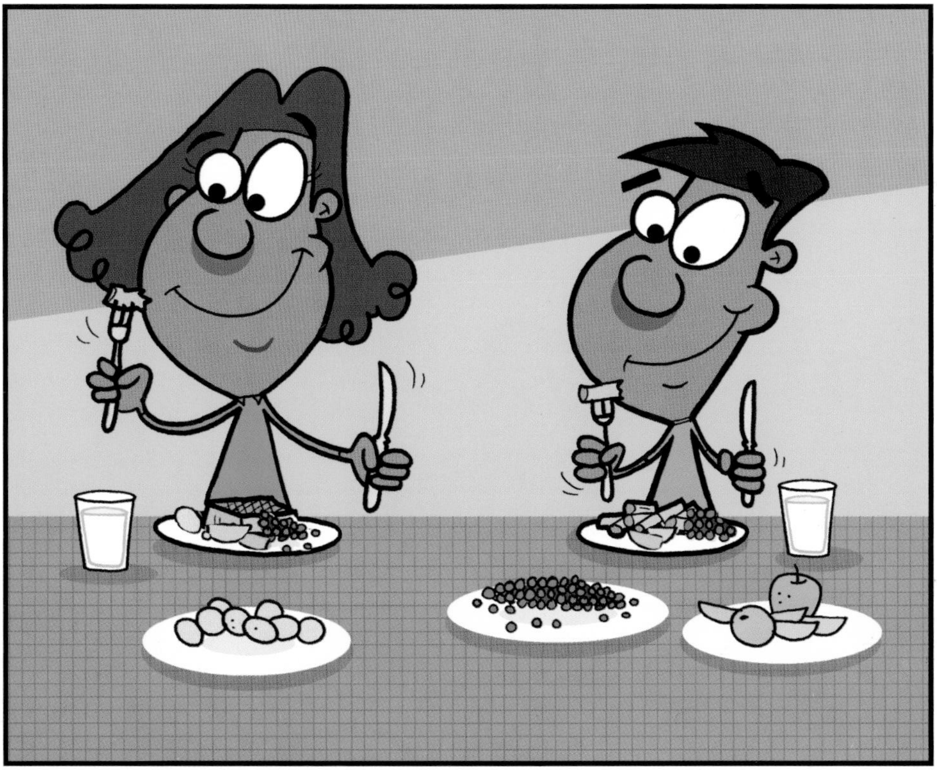

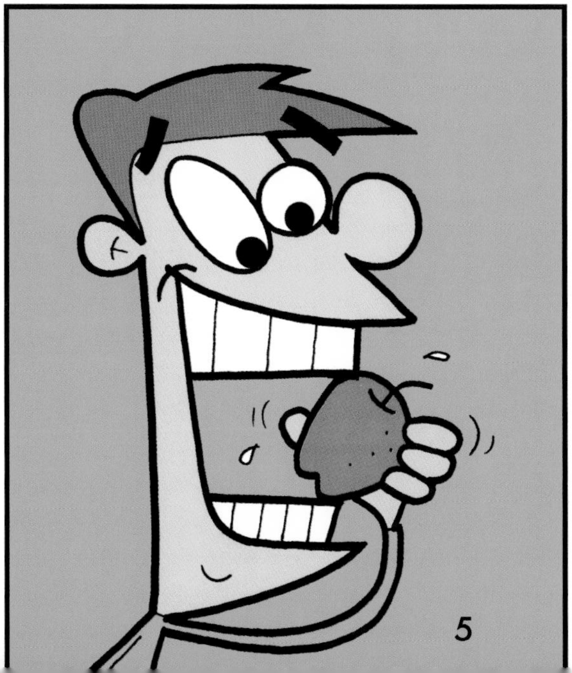

The red section stands for the fruit group. Fruits and vegetables should fill half of your plate.

Liven up meals and snack time with fruit. It's naturally sweet and healthy.

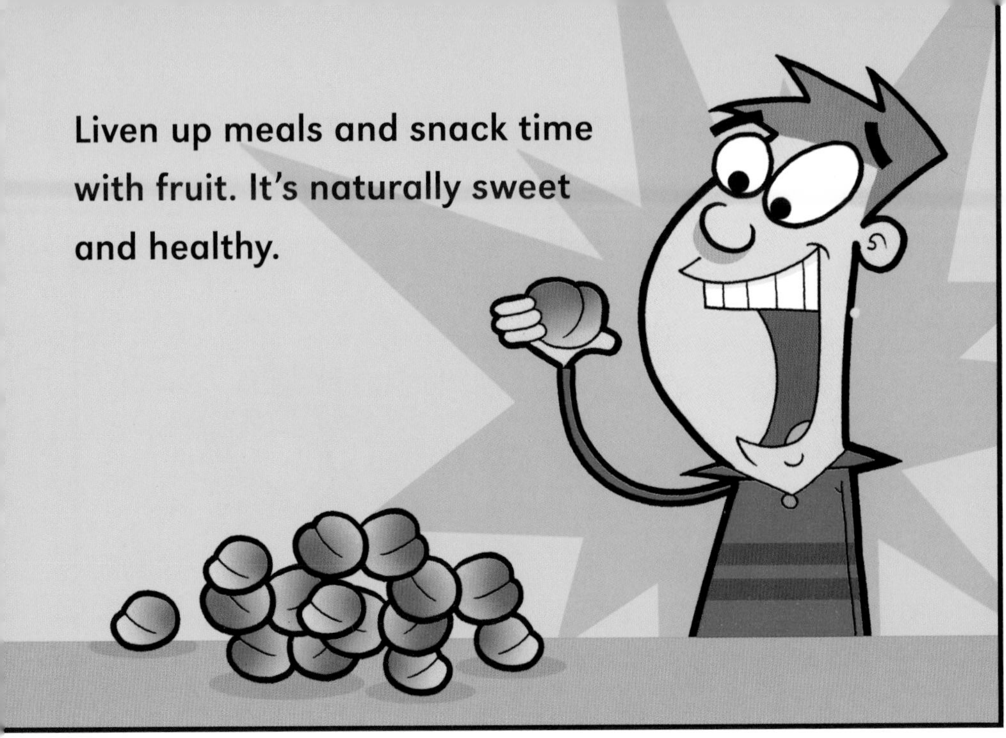

Breakfast is extra tasty when you add fruit.

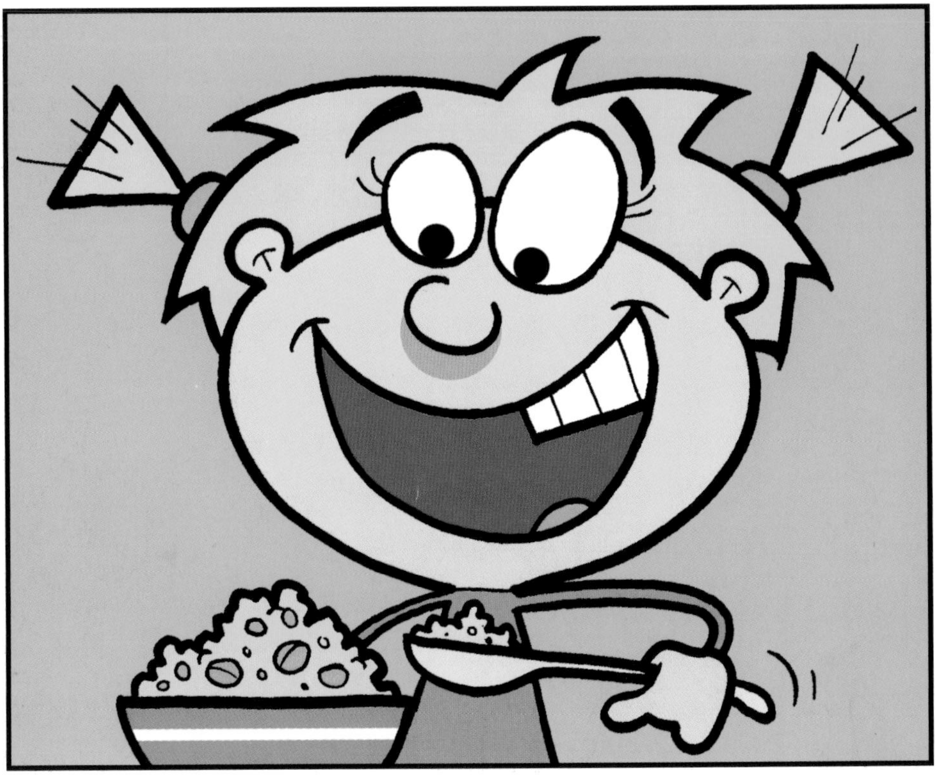

Fruit also makes a great snack or dessert.

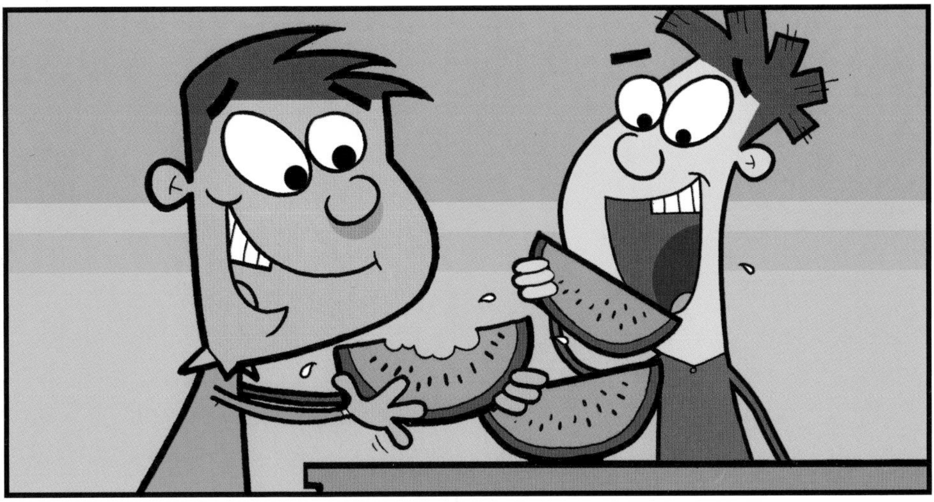

You can squeeze fruit juice yourself.

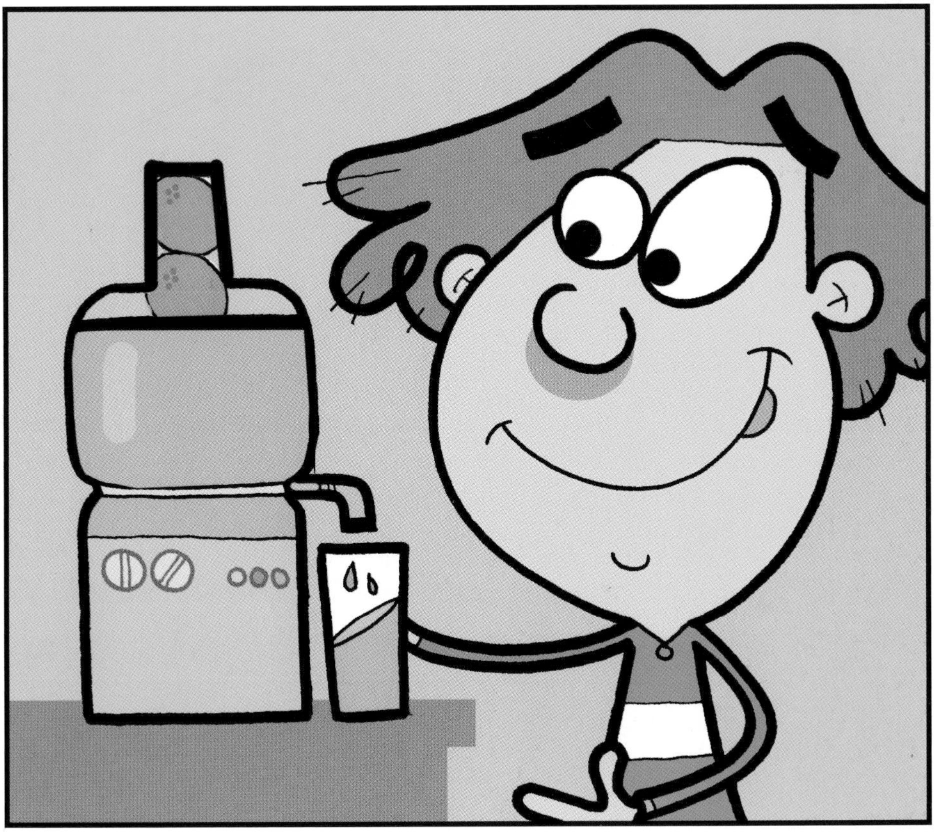

Fruit comes in a rainbow of colors. Eat different colors for good health.

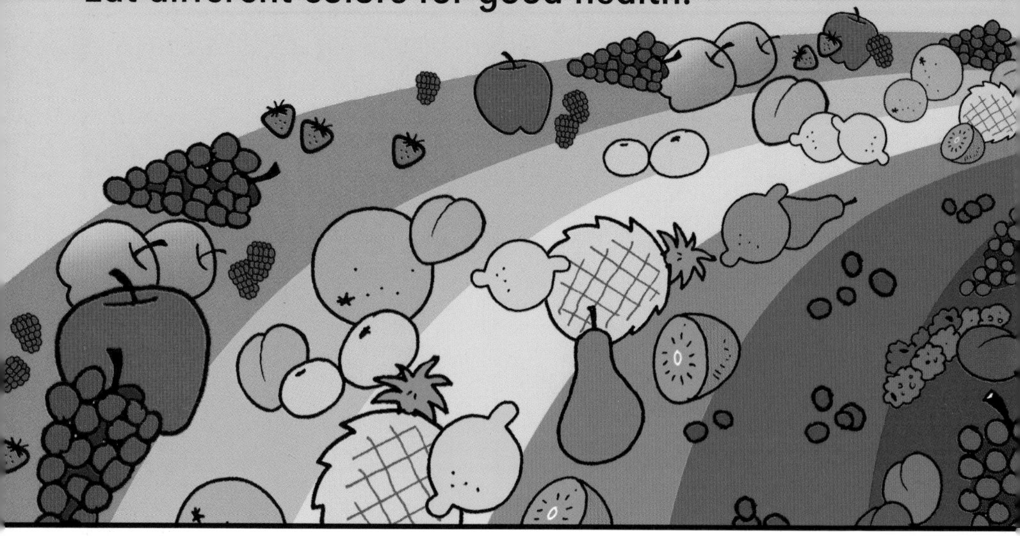

Apples, strawberries, and watermelon are red fruits.

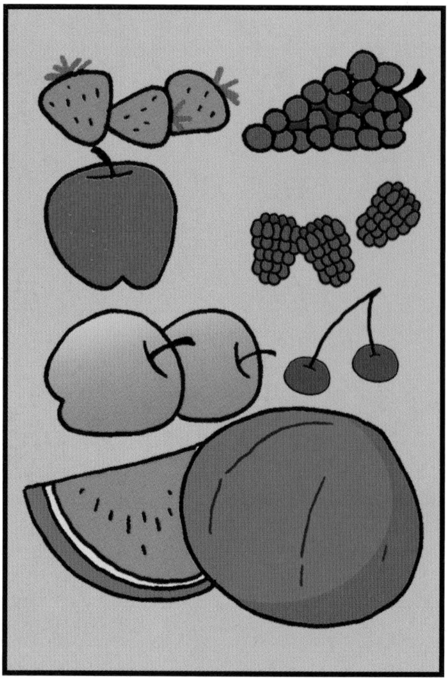

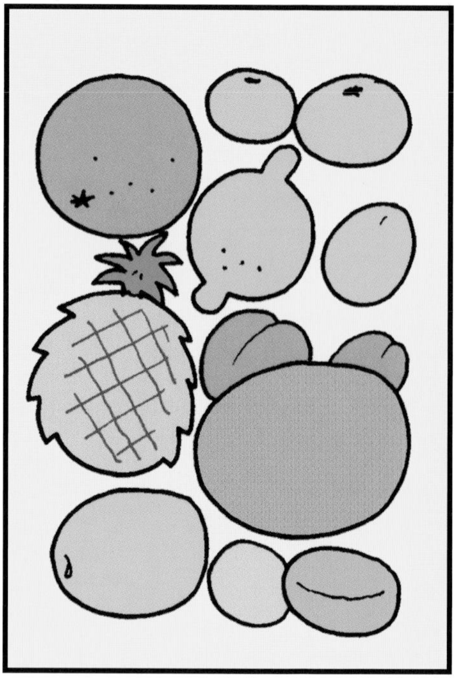

Orange and yellow fruits include peaches, pineapples, and oranges.

You might like green fruits such as honeydew or kiwi.

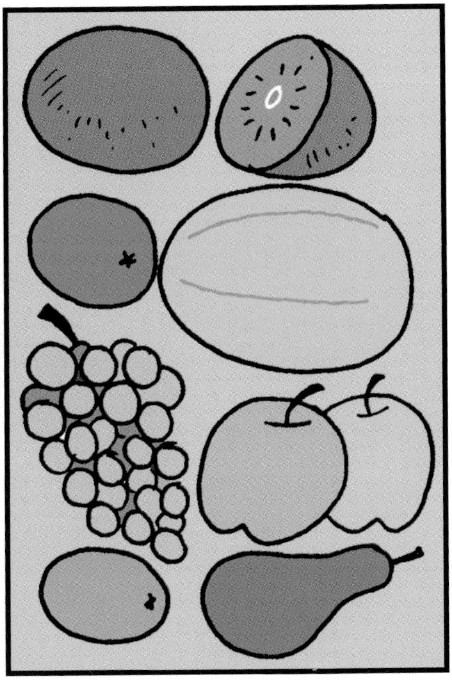

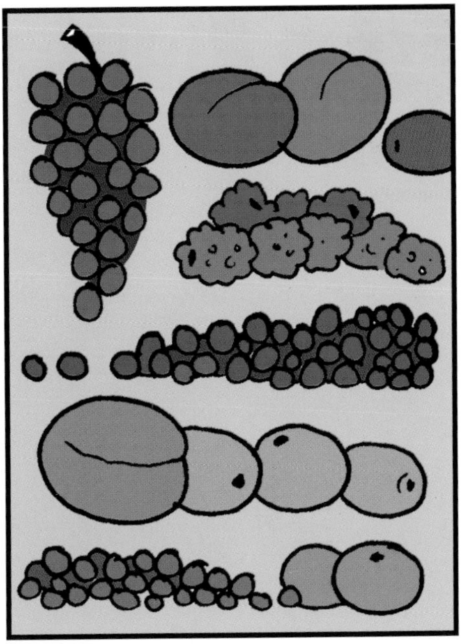

Blackberries and plums are blue and purple fruits.

Bananas are a white fruit with a yellow skin.

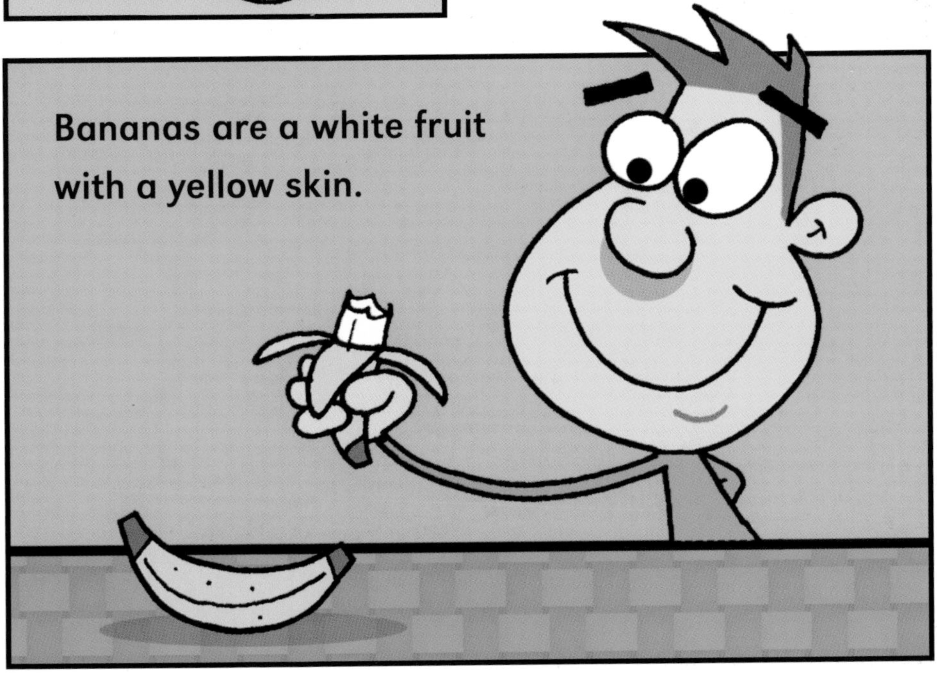

From Plant to Plate

Fruit grows from flowers on trees, bushes, and vines.

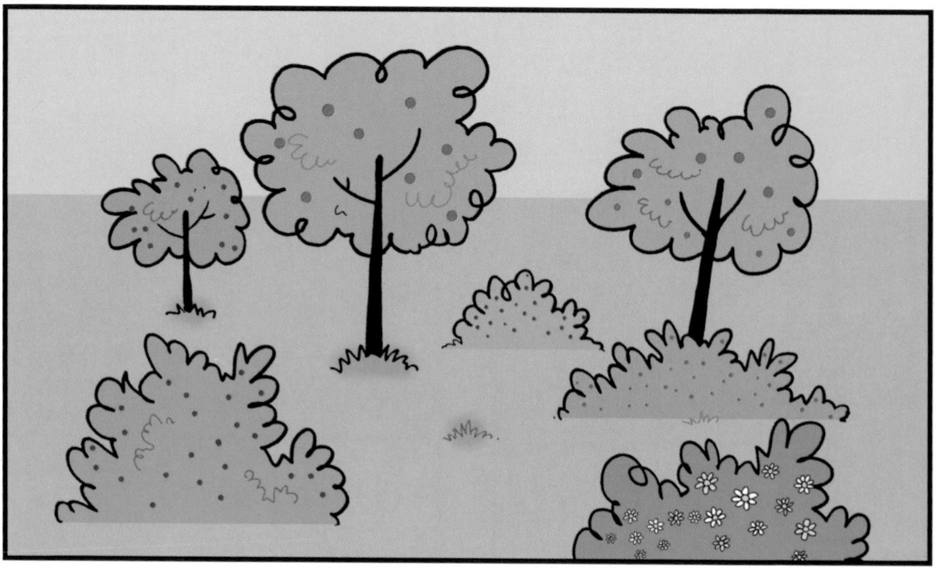

When bees visit flowers, pollen sticks to their legs.

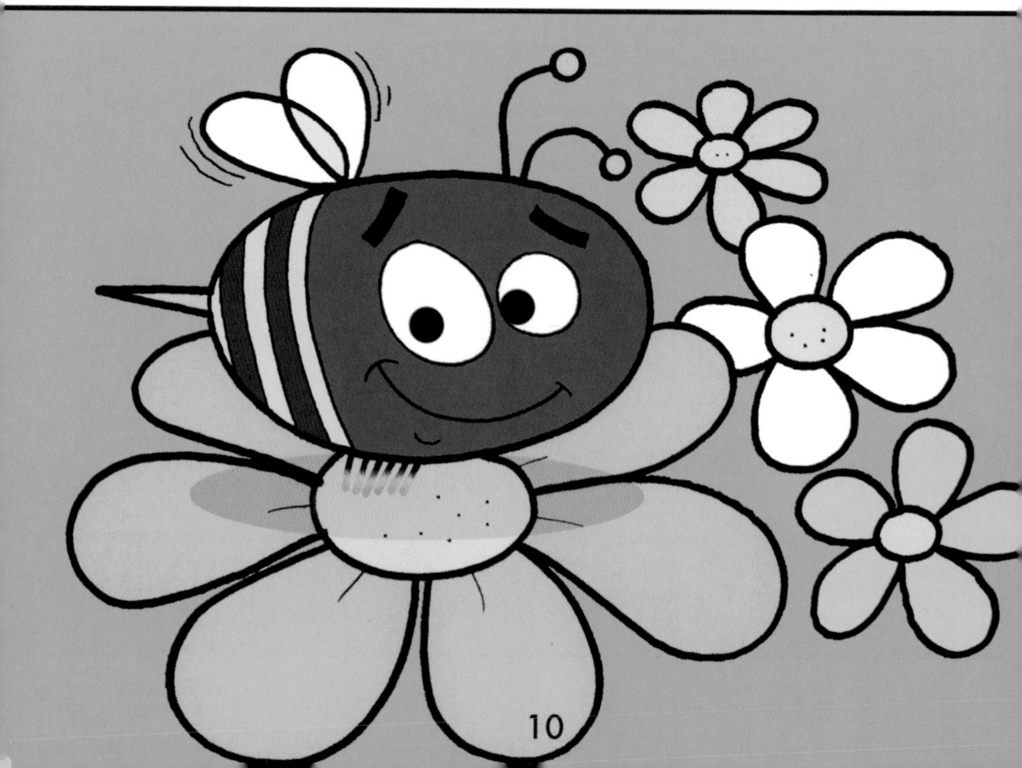

The bees spread the pollen to other flowers they visit. Flowers need pollen to grow fruit.

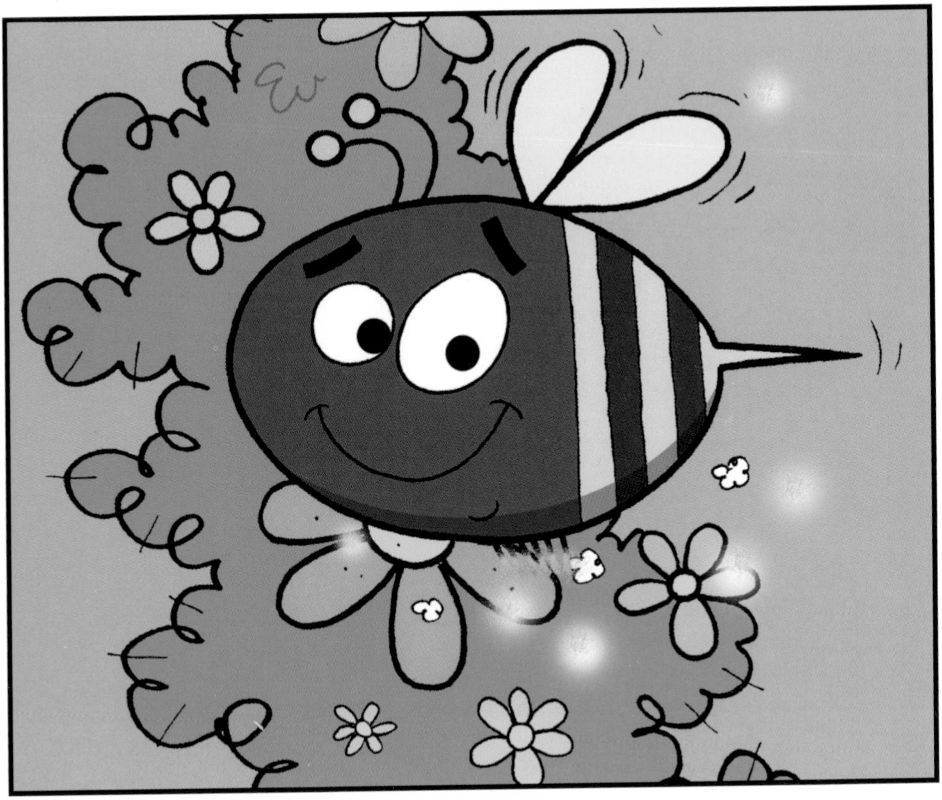

Fruit has seeds. Birds and other animals eat fruit and spread the seeds around.

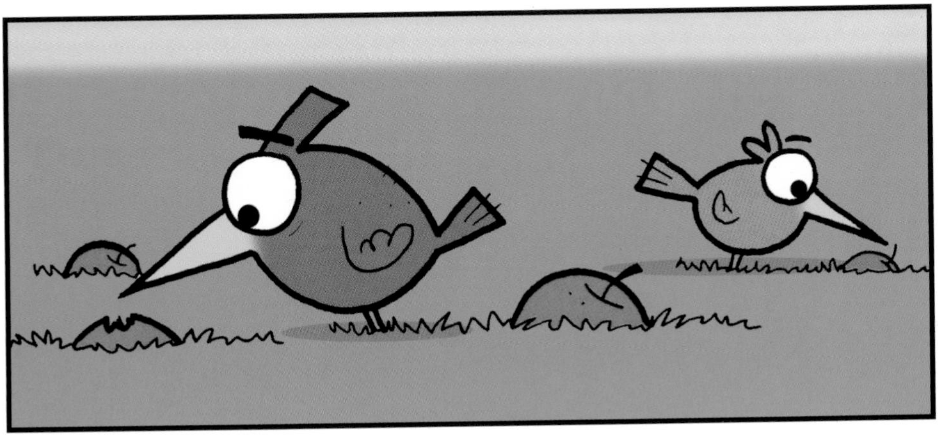

Most fruit plants need a lot of sun.

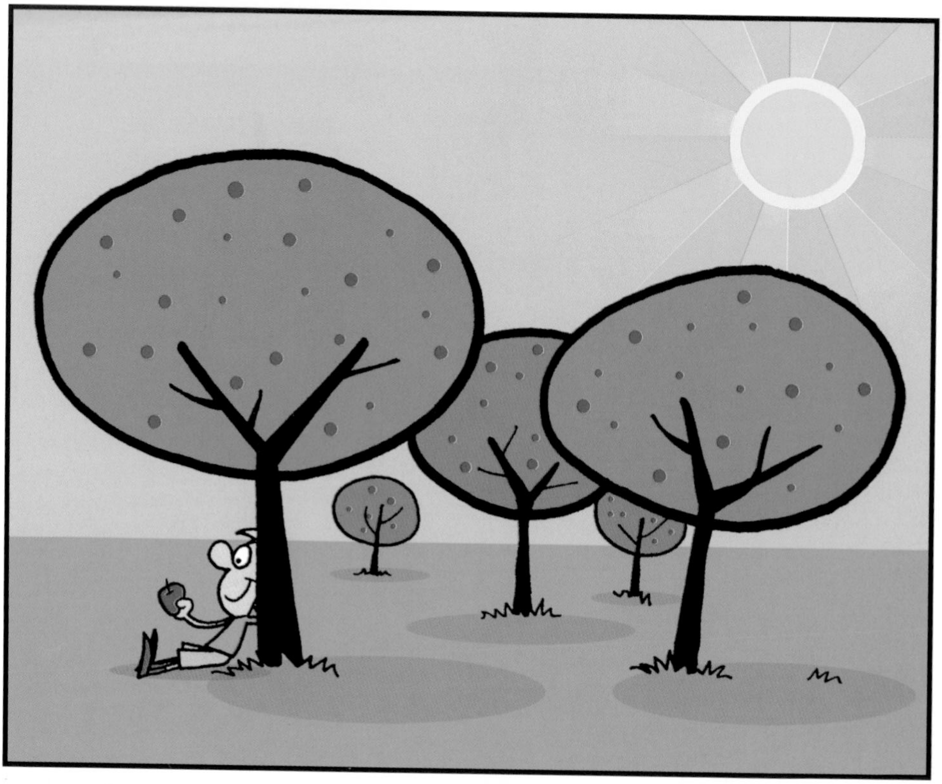

Some fruit grows with less sun.

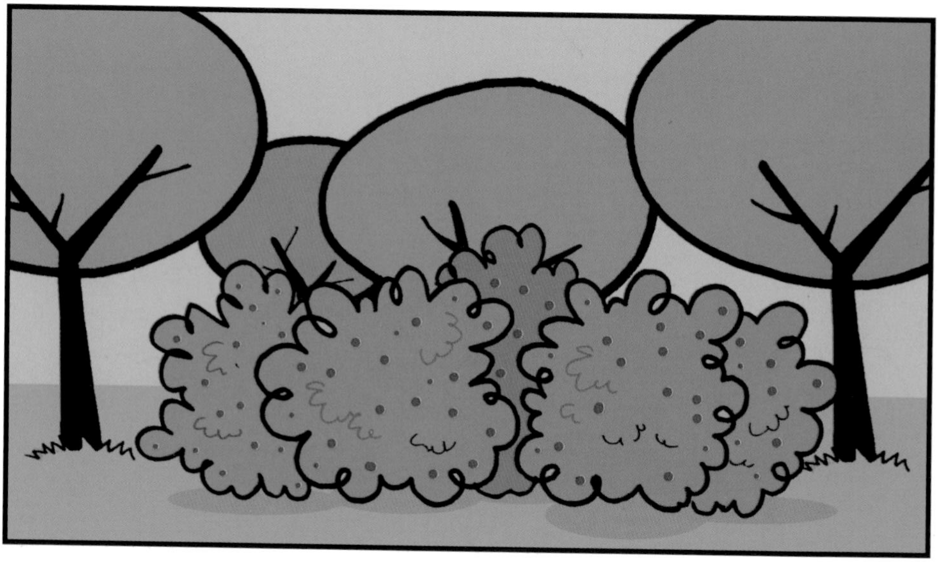

Some people grow fruit in their yards.

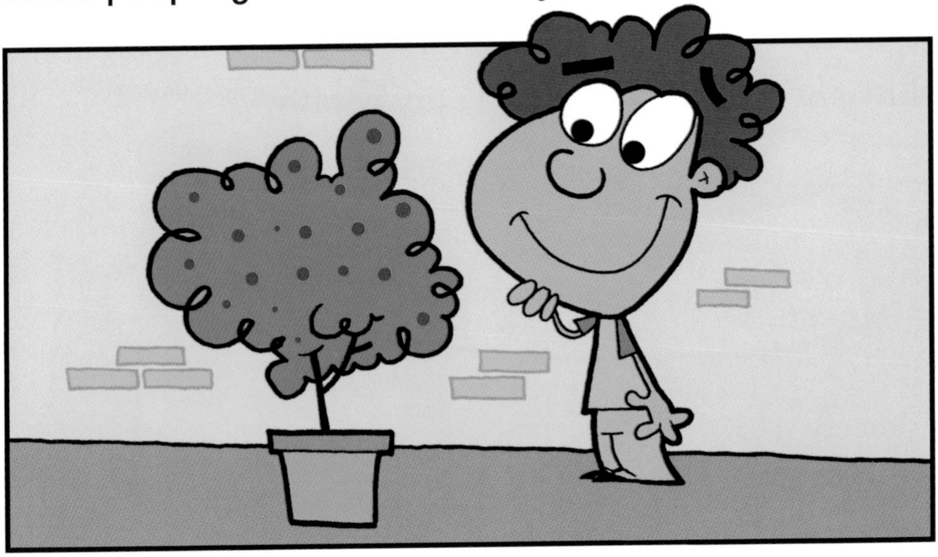

Apple, peach, and plum trees grow in larger areas called orchards.

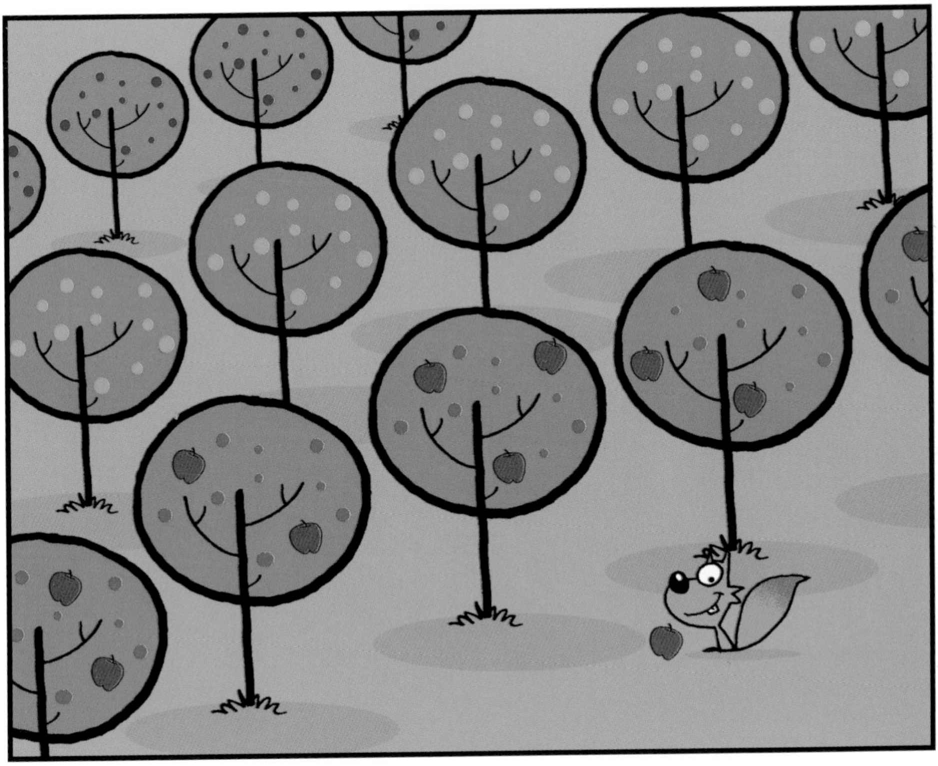

Healthy Eating

Nutrients in fruits help you stay healthy.

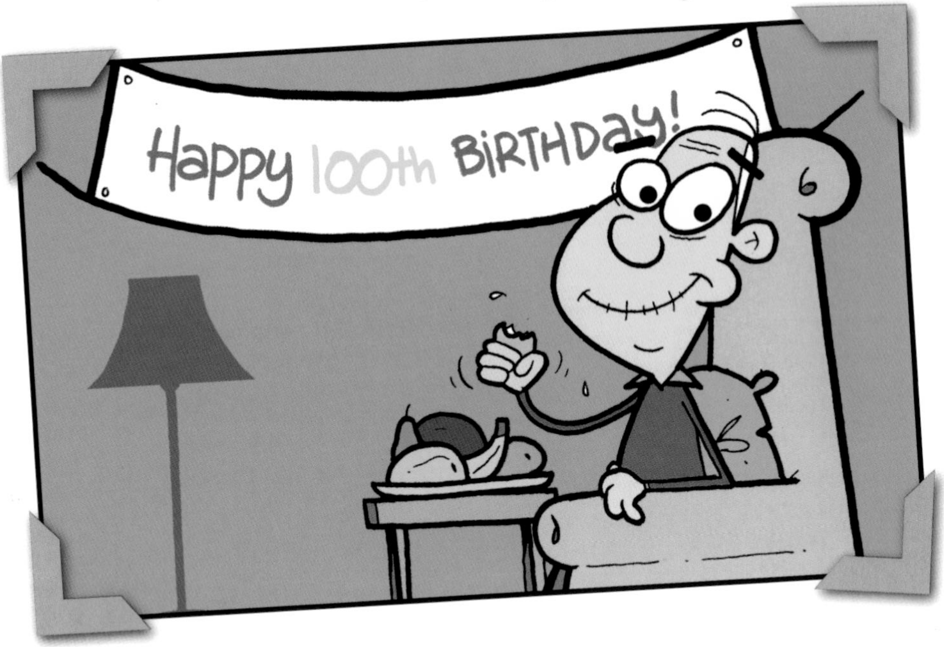
Happy 100th BiRTHDay!

Watermelon, bananas, and cantaloupe have potassium to keep your heart pumping.

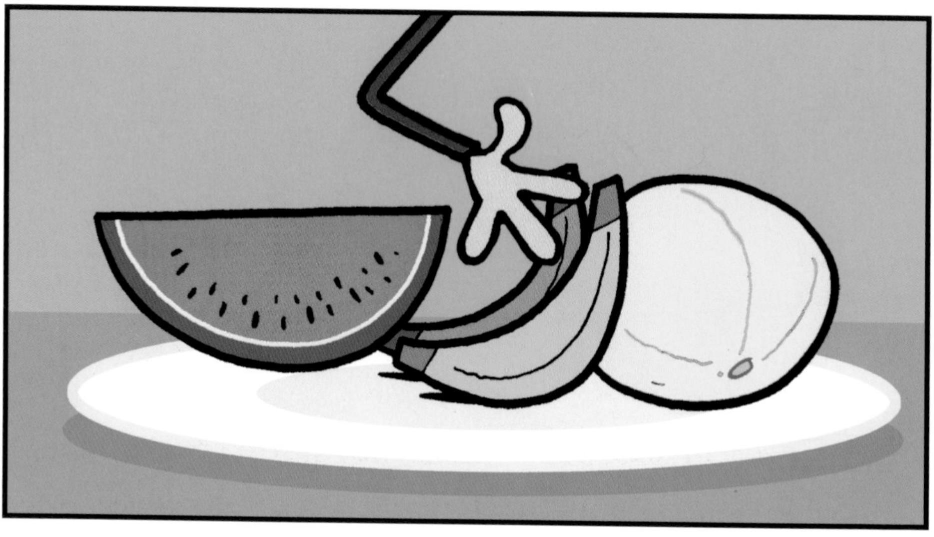

Vitamin C helps heal cuts and keeps teeth and gums healthy. Oranges, pineapples, and strawberries have a lot of vitamin C.

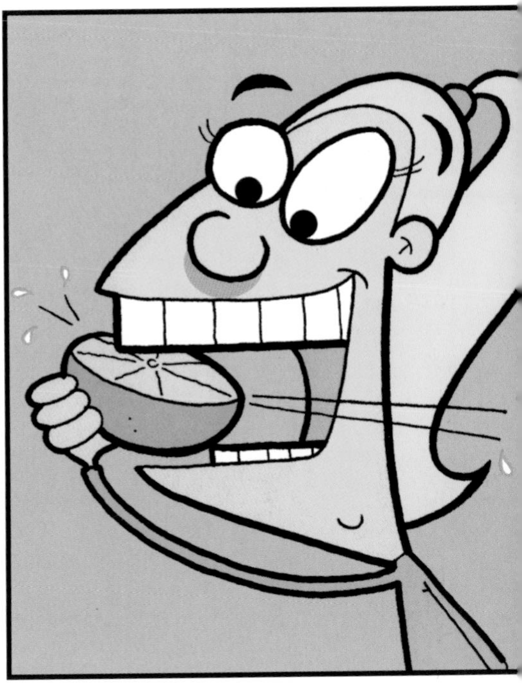

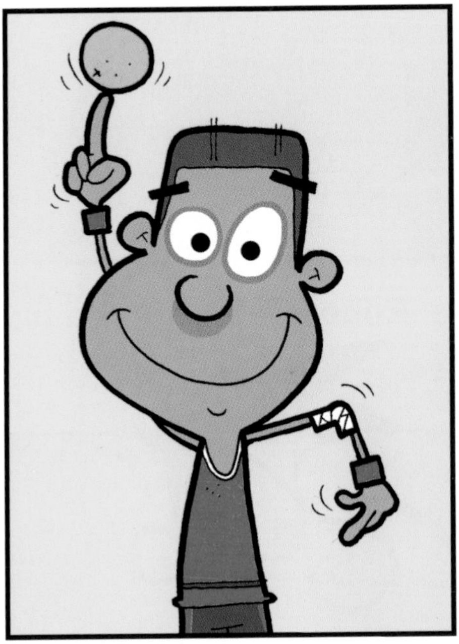

Vitamin A helps your eyes, skin, and hair stay healthy. Watermelon, grapefruit, and mangoes have vitamin A.

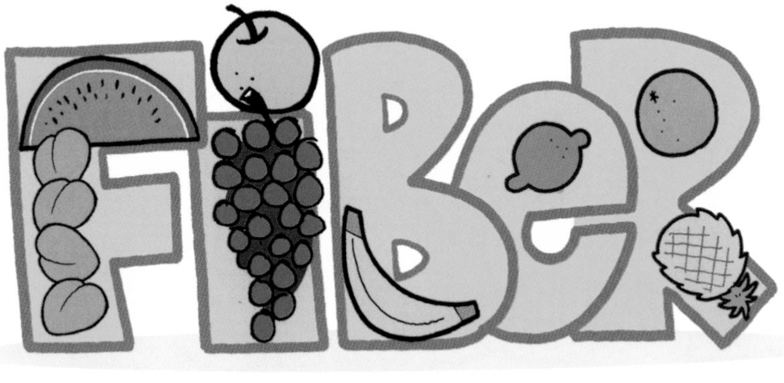
FIBER

Fruit is a good source of fiber. Your body needs fiber every day. Fiber helps food move through your body.

You can enjoy fruit year-round.

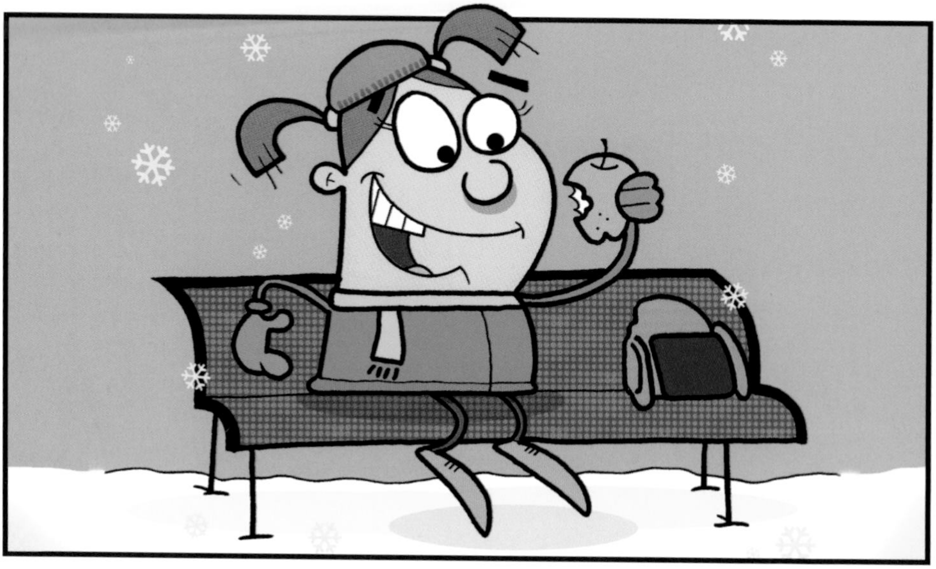

Some fruit is available in cans. Choose fruit packed in water or 100 percent fruit juice.

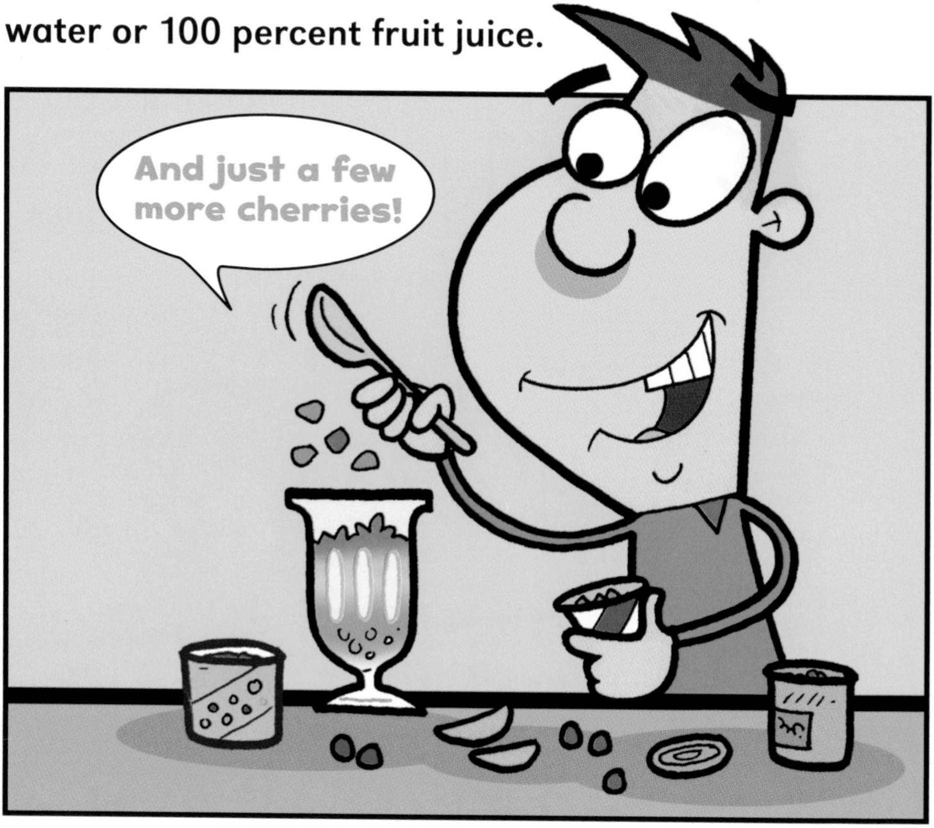
And just a few more cherries!

Small containers of fruit are great with lunch.

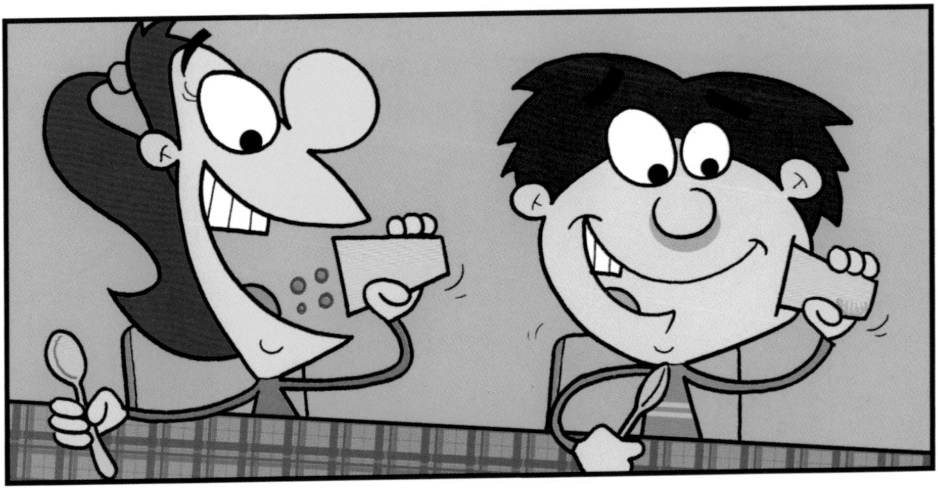

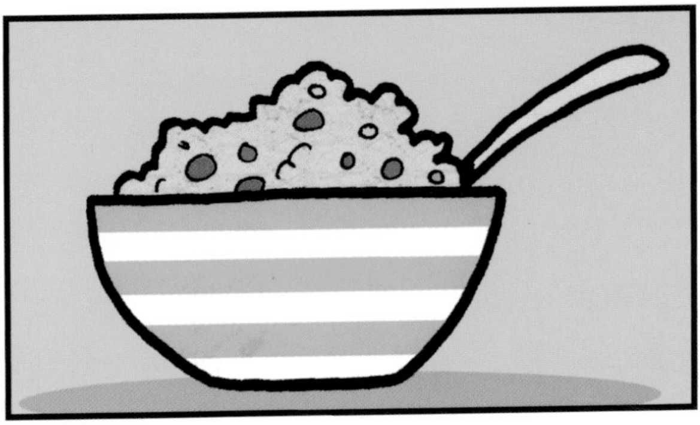

Dried fruit is tasty on oatmeal.

Frozen fruit and low-fat yogurt make great smoothies.

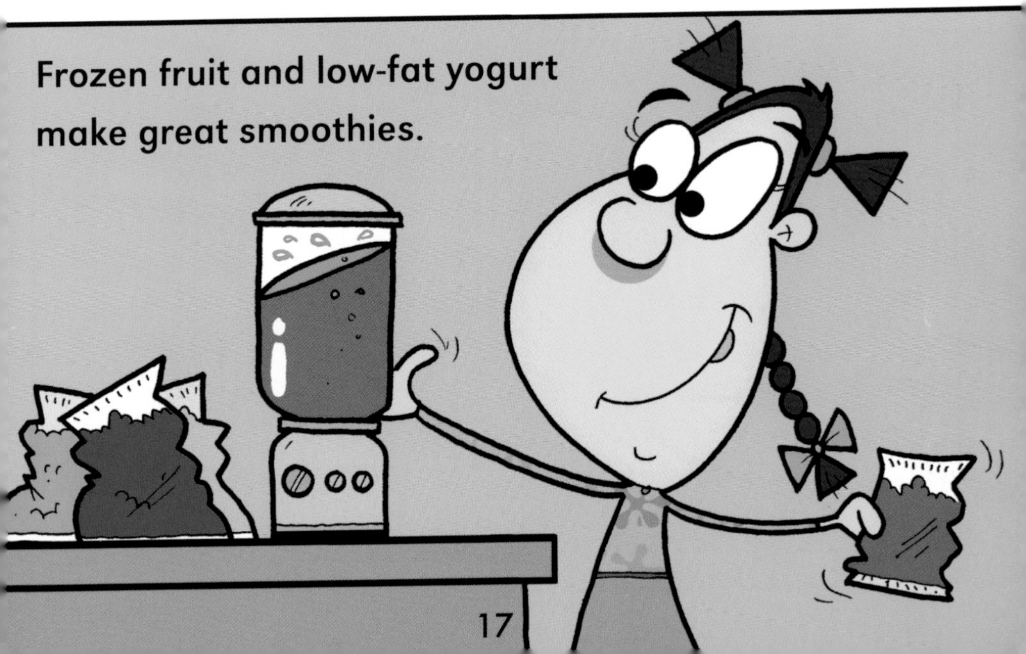

Kids need two to three ½-cup servings of fruit every day.

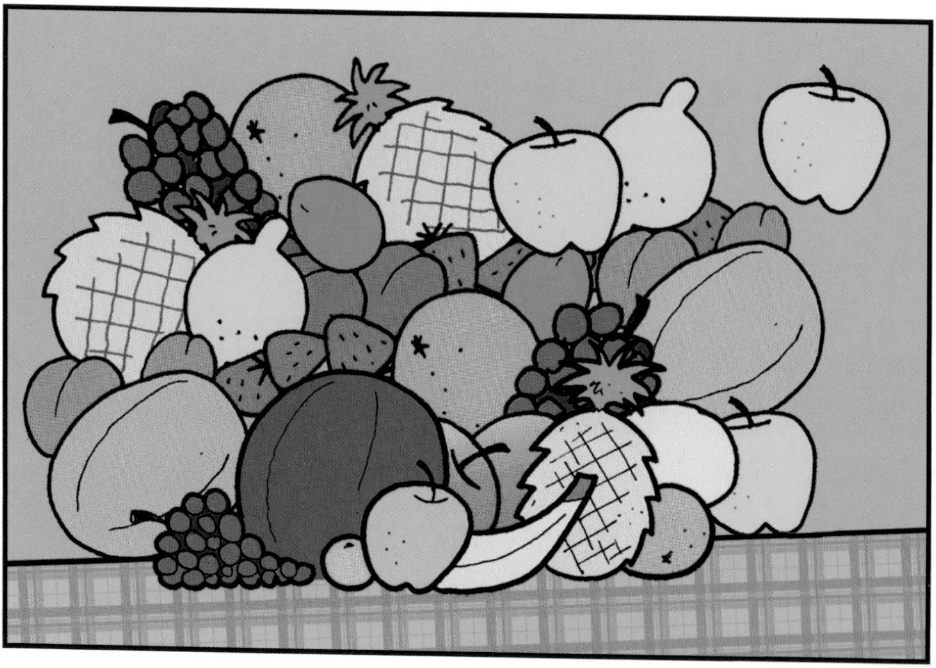

One small banana or one small orange make one serving of fruit.

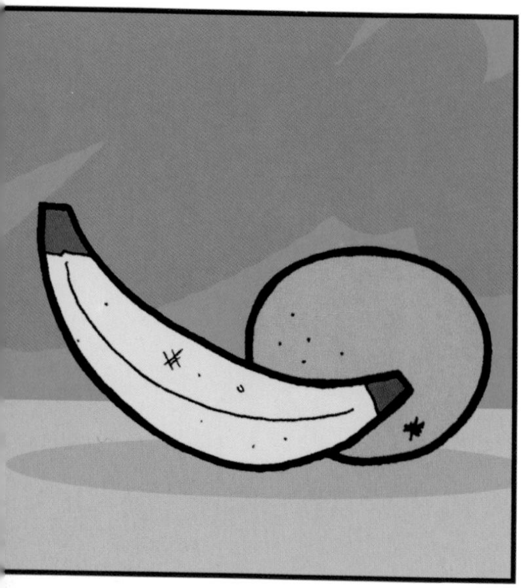

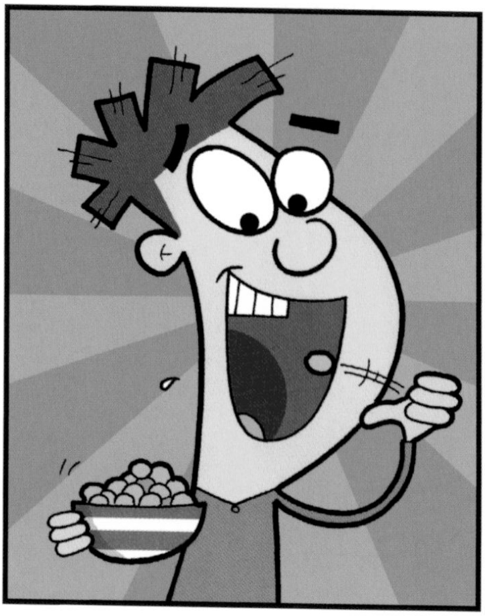

Sixteen grapes make another serving.

Get in another serving with ½ cup of strawberries.

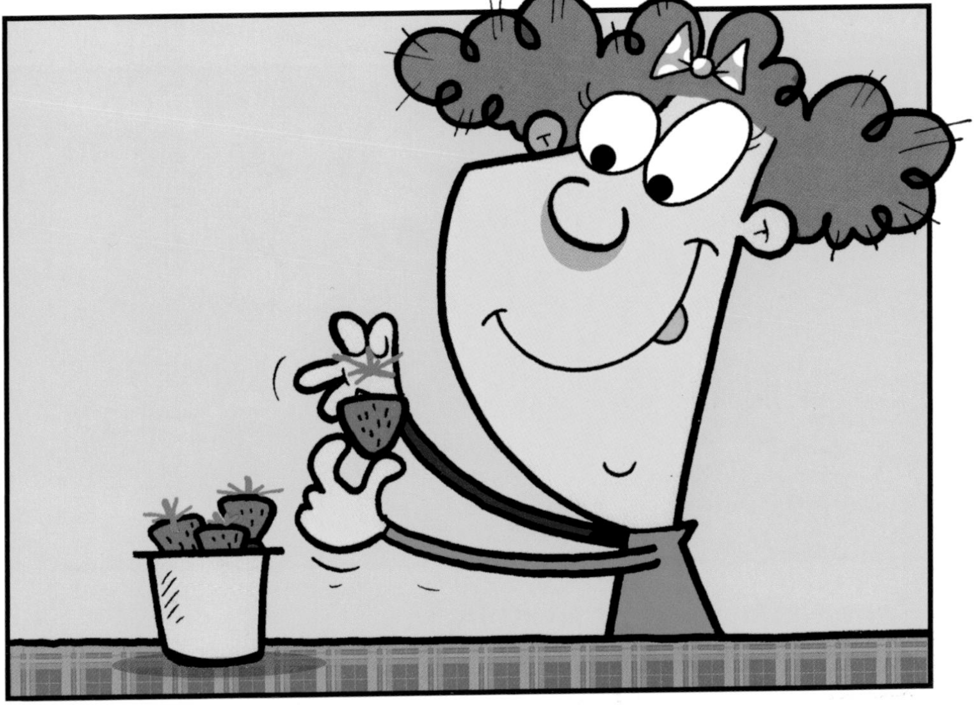

A ½ cup of sliced apple
also makes one serving.

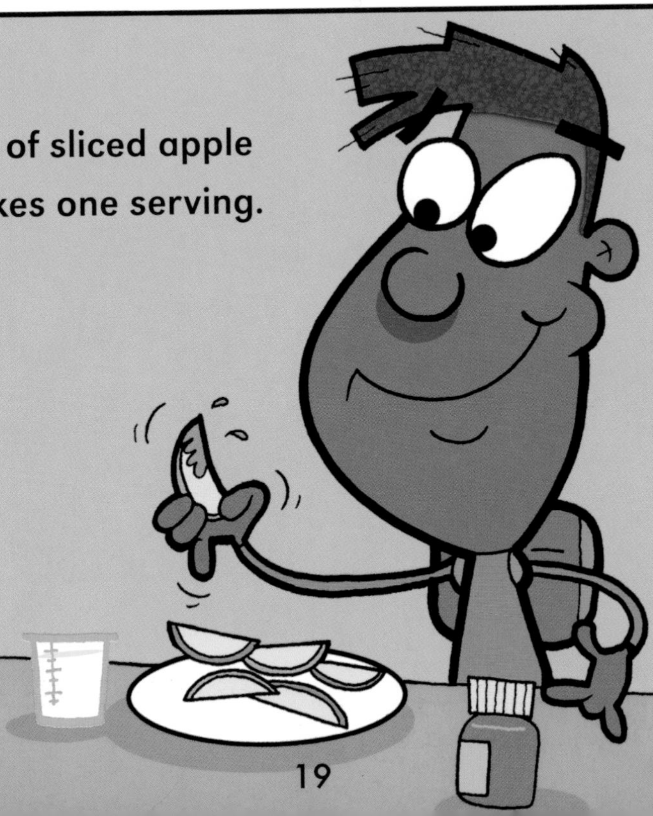

There are many fruits to choose from.
Try something new!

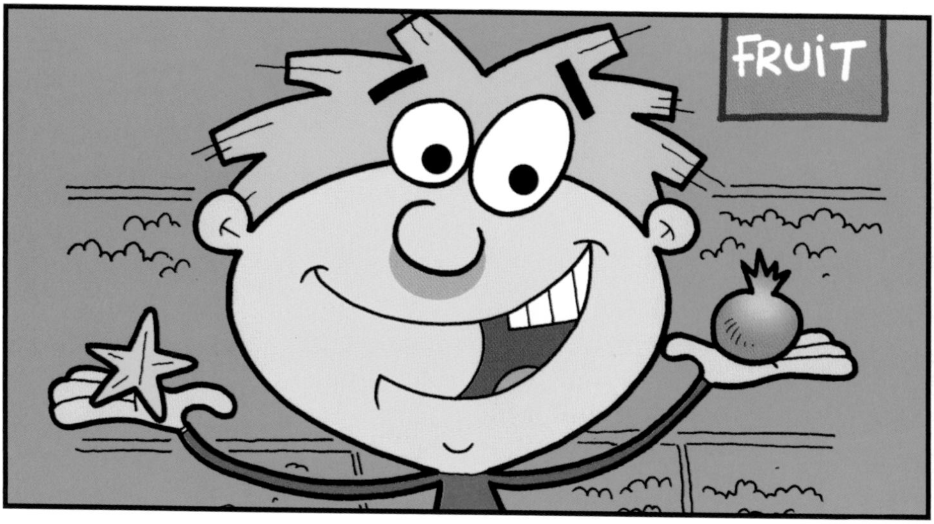
FRUIT

Mangoes first came from India.
Kiwis came from China.

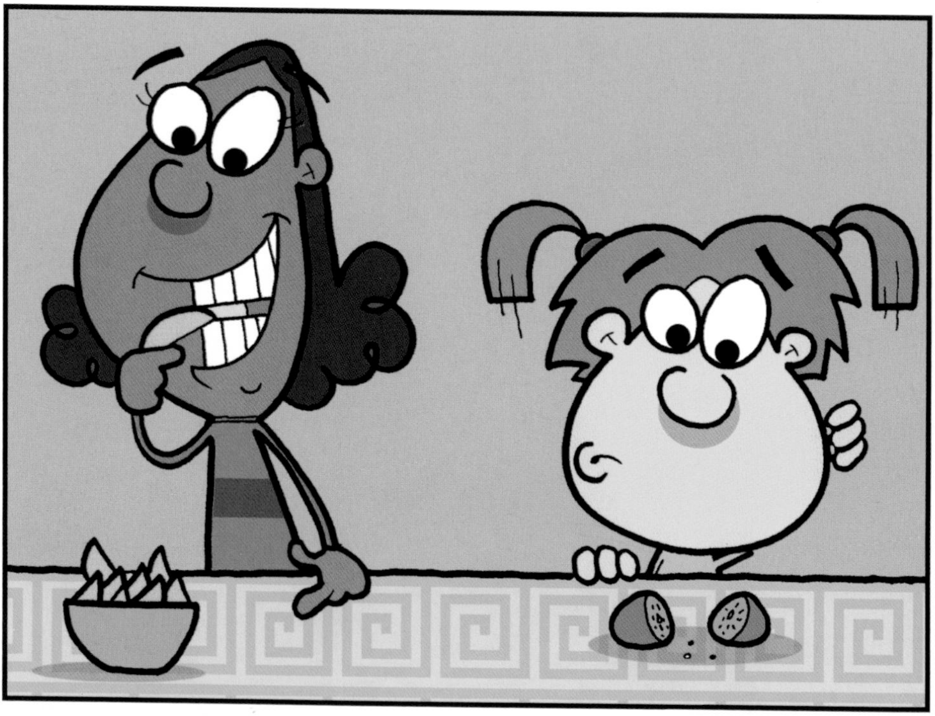

A rainbow fruit salad is a healthy treat for the whole family.

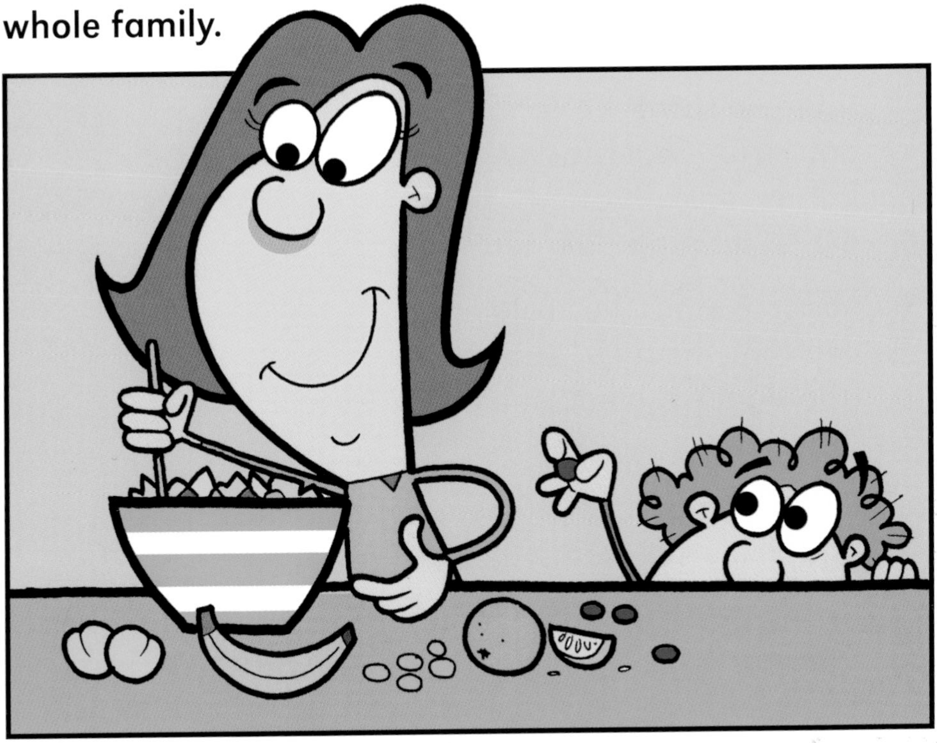

What fruit will you eat today?

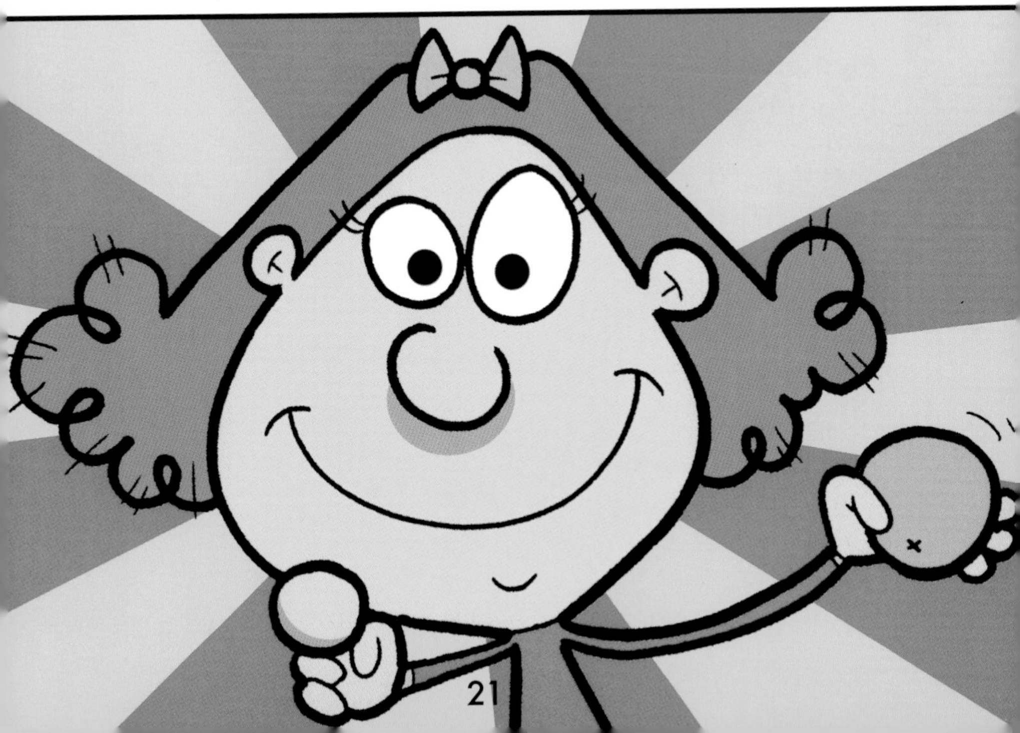

Glossary

fiber—a part of foods such as bread and fruit that passes through the body but is not digested; fiber helps food move through the intestines

MyPlate—an illustrated guide that explains healthy eating and shows what a balanced meal should look like

nutrient—a substance needed by a living thing to stay healthy; vitamins and minerals are nutrients

orchard—a field or farm where fruit trees are grown

pollen—a powder made by flowers to help them create new seeds

potassium—a silver-white chemical element found in foods such as bananas and potatoes

serving—a recommended amount of food or drink

vitamin—a nutrient that helps keep people healthy

Read More

Adams, Julia. *Fruits.* Good Food. New York: PowerKids Press, 2011.

Burstein, John. *Fabulous Fruits.* Slim Goodbody's Nutrition Edition. New York: Crabtree Pub., 2010.

Tourville, Amanda Doering. *Fuel the Body: Eating Well.* How to be Healthy! Minneapolis: Picture Window Books, 2009.

Internet Sites

FactHound offers a safe, fun way to find Internet sites related to this book. All of the sites on FactHound have been researched by our staff.

Here's all you do:

Visit *www.facthound.com*

Type in this code: 9781429660907

Check out projects, games and lots more at
www.capstonekids.com

Index

MyPlate and Healthy Eating

TITLES IN THIS SET:

The Delicious Dairy Group

The Fantastic Fruit Group

The Great Grains Group

Healthy Snacks, Healthy You!

The Incredible Vegetable Group

The Powerful Protein Group

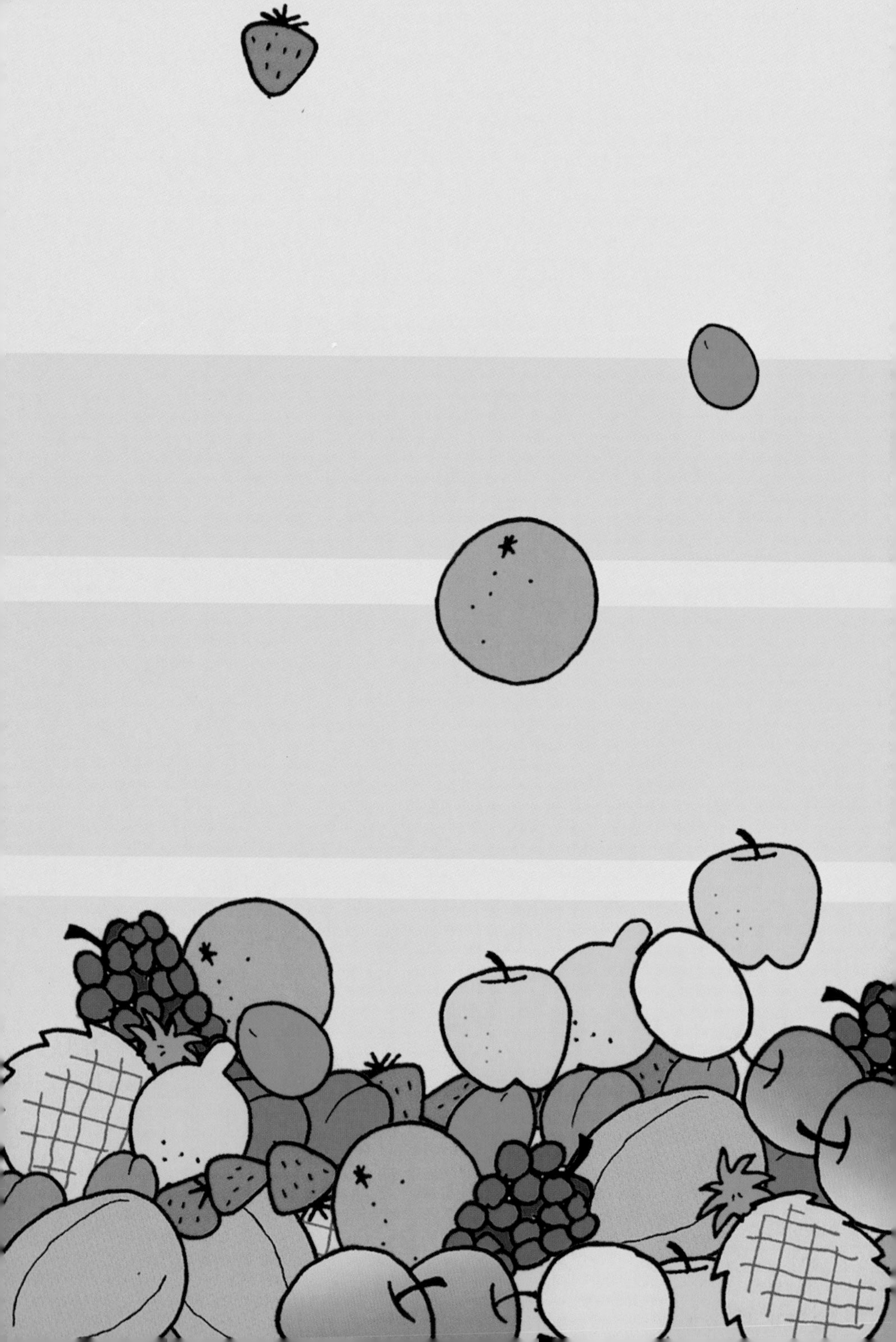

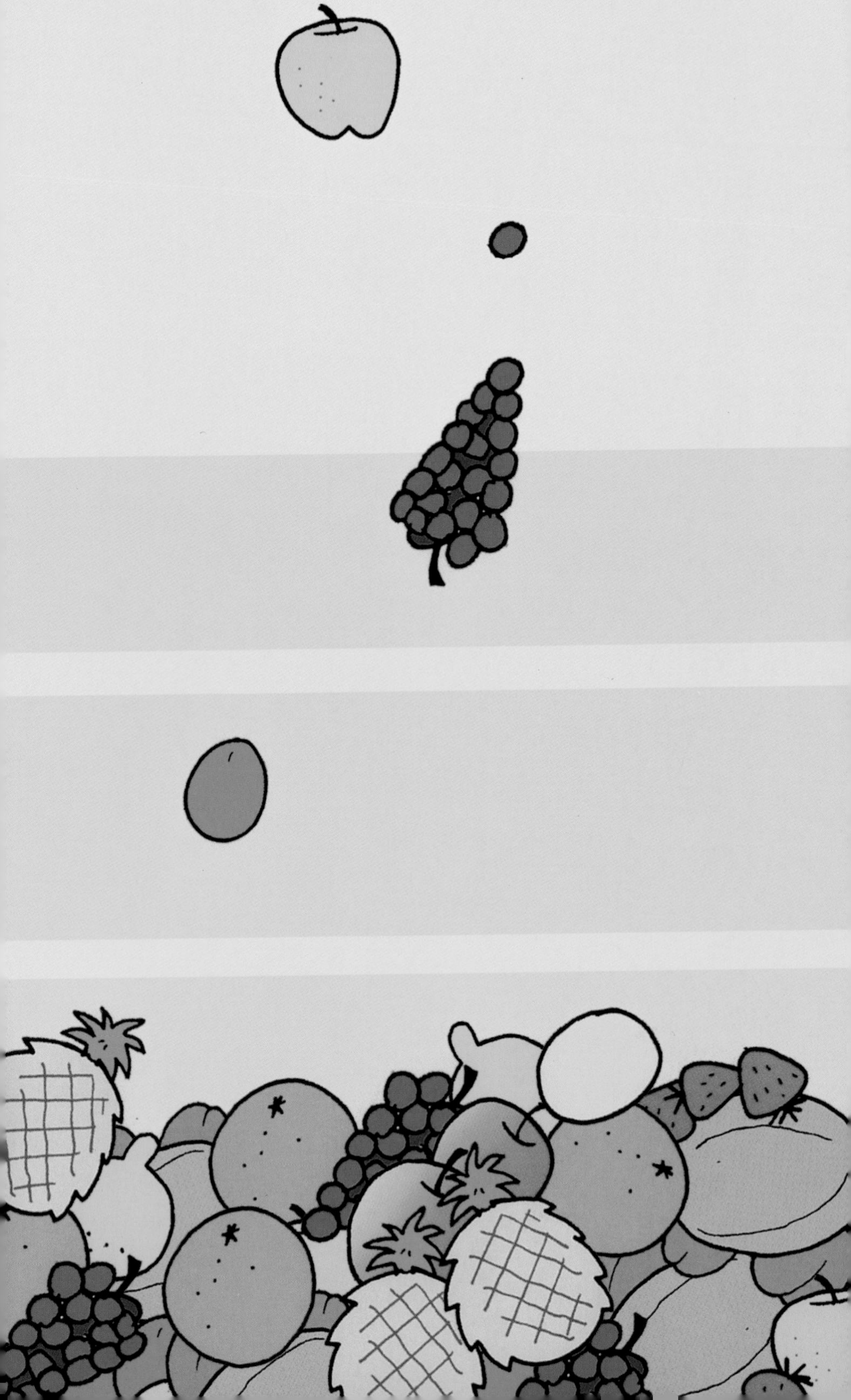